Wake up and cut the puppet strings!

Dedicated to the truth seekers and truth speakers.

These are crazy times in the world and it's time for people to see that they are just being used by a system that doesn't care about them but only what they can use you for. Tax dollars, spreading lies and hate, you are being used and it's time you all woke up and take off the blinders, accept reality, and cut the puppet strings! Everything I'm coming at you with is 100% truth, all researched. But first a little flashback.

Ever since I can remember I saw the world for what it was. I look to peace and love but see a deep sinister power at work. I was raised during the Vietnam war. I lived in a middle-class area in a decent size midwestern city, and my neighborhood was full of World War 2 and Korean war veterans. So, when the Vietnam war was raging, it was just another "good old-fashioned war."

It started out with "advisers" to train the South Vietnamese army and that started in 1955. Then we supplied them with equipment to fight. Bombs, helicopters, guns, ammo. Because we needed to stop the threat of Communism. If we didn't stop it there, it would soon be over here in the USA!

Nightly we'd hear it all on the news, daily the newspapers (remember those?) would fall at our door and that was all that it seemed to be. We'd hear how we were gaining ground and how many enemies were dead. By killing more of them then us we were winning, I guess. The old veterans loved it. And everyone I know was buying into it because the media told them to.

But then came the day reality hit close to home. A black sedan pulled up to the neighbor kids house on the corner. He was a draftee in the Army and was over in Nam. Two men got out and presented his dad with a letter and a flag. We didn't understand it, just being kids and all, but he was killed at the age of 19 by the Vietcong. Now the war had a face and a name close to us. And everything for me changed. We knew what happened. We looked around at the older kids, close to draft age, and wondered if it would be them someday. And we wondered why. And then we wondered what would happen to us if the so-called war kept going.

That family soon moved away, and we never saw or heard from them again. The old veterans called him a hero. Some of the younger people questioned his death. And I had to wonder why he died and what the real reason was.

Many of us in my neighborhood were close to being 18. Would they go from playing baseball and kickball with us to coming home in a box? People started to worry. Protestors were out in droves, even though when the war first started most US citizens were in approval of it. But now we young kids had to wonder why?

In 1975 when the last troops left, I watched as Saigon fell to the North Vietnamese, the enemy. We had left after 20 years 58,220 Americans dead, a reported 168 billion dollars spent on the war, and over 2 million Vietnamese soldiers and civilian's dead from the war. And for what? A big sacrifice supposedly to stop the spread of communism but we failed.

Vietnam, and Indo China, became a full Communist country. And still is. But did it spread? Did it take over America? I still see us with free (kind of) democratic elections. So, I began to question things starting with the government and the media. We had been lied to and I don't like much being lied to. It is an insult to my intelligence to be expected to believe everything I'm told. I was fully woken at an incredibly young age.

I am not a crook.

To top things off we had a President, Tricky Dick Nixon, who said he was not a crook. He told us so and we all know Presidents don't lie. And we all knew if it was in the paper or on the news or if we learned it in school, it must be the absolute truth.

We are indoctrinated to believe what we are told at a young age by our families, whether it's by them, or in the churches, or the media. Shut up and listen is what I was always being told. Don't question anything. Believe it, it's true.

But then you would hear about a minister preaching about the evils of doing immoral things getting caught doing those things himself. Or a teacher. Or even the president who avoided impeachment by resigning. So, who can you trust? You find out most everyone is lying and being hypocrites. And you find out you yourself are being trained to grow up and live a lie.

Well, I wasn't going to fall for that, and I started to question all that I had learned. I was a reader already, but I became a big bookworm. They knew me at my local library quite well, although they didn't really care much for me. Young kids don't belong in a library reading what I was reading. I started digging into military history, world history, government, and books about the people who built our country. And my mind was blown!

No two books ever agree, some were very pro, and some were very against. Many exposed people for how they really were. My library was a Carnegie library set up by the Scottish philanthropist Andrew Carnegie. And even he had had controversies despite giving away a ton of his wealth, but that's no surprise since the wealthy get special privileges. Always have, always will.

I started reading old newspapers, books written by people in other countries, by communist, I even read Mein Kompf just to get a worldly view of what was going on around us. Of course, now you can't find a copy of that book that is actually straight written by the author, Adolf Hitler, a man I do not respect or like but at the same time I am amazed how someone like him could have got many millions of civilized people to follow him blindly and have them all be full of rage and hatred. It's almost like they don't want people to read that book anymore even though it is very historical and probably should be read by everybody.

Almost every book had an agenda. An agenda for the cause they believed was the right cause, the only true cause. And many people are always searching for someone to follow, something to believe in. So, who do we decide is correct? It's hard to figure out and even harder today.

In the 60's growing up I was bombarded daily on our 3 tv networks and the cities only newspaper on what was truly going on in the world. I grew up with Martin Luther King getting shot, civil rights riots, the Detroit riots (I still have newspaper clipping from those riots), the so called "Manson Cult Killings," kings and leaders getting shot and taken out, then it moved into the 70's with Kent State and so much more. As a young kid I was told this was how the world worked and always worked, but I knew it was wrong! I knew there was more that we as a public we weren't being shown or told. Don't peek behind the curtain, you'll see the truth.

We were being acclimated to the ills of society and told "that's just the way it is, don't speak out or try to change it, just deal with it."

The schools were teaching us the victor's way of American and World history but not what really happened and why. The media told you this was the way, that's it, accept it, go to work, pay taxes, and question nothing.

Then came Watergate. As a kid we were repeating our parent's words, that Nixon was a great president. We'd chant "Nixon, Nixon he's our man, McGovern belongs in the garbage can." We didn't know why. We were doing what we were taught. We were programmed. So were our parents. Children learn what they live.

But on June 17, 1972, that was all we started hearing about. I couldn't understand why he did what he did at that time. I mean, he beat McGovern 520 electoral votes to 17! That's crazy. And yet he got himself in hot water and it cost him everything.

Years later I realized just how much a scammer, liar, and hustler Nixon was. The dam was open, and the truth was flowing through it and many American people were finally seeing reality at last.

The Truth Will Set You Free

In the Holy Bible, John wrote that the truth would set you free. No, it won't. The truth will get you locked up, beaten, or killed. It will cost you everything you own. You see, big government doesn't like the truth and they don't want you to know it or like it. They feel they are the only ones able to handle the truth. That's why there has always been so many coverups with alien contact and more. That's why they spread the lies and hate and keep division going. Divide and conquer, the oldest trick in the book.

In 1952 Project Bluebook was started by the United States Airforce to do systematic studies on Unidentified Flying Objects. They closed the project in 1969. They researched approximately 12,618 sightings reported to them. Only 701 remain unidentified. That's a lot of swamp gas!

Yet they make movies about aliens, space, and extra-terrestrial contact constantly. Do you know why? Not just for easy money but because it's all real! Are you so vain to think in this vast universe we are alone? Do you really think there are no other beings in the universe? They want you to believe that. They say, "you need carbon or oxygen to have life." Maybe we do but others might not.

And why do they shove this down your throat? Because they have an agenda. They are trying to desensitize you to what's out there so when it happens, you'll be okay with it. Our government has been working with aliens for many years now.

Roswell New Mexico, July 8, 1947, the Roswell Daily Record newspaper headline reads "RAAF captures flying saucer on ranch in Roswell region." This was big time! Bodies were recovered, strange metal like composites were recovered, and many of the witnesses were military. But immediately our government covered it up. Then in the mid 1990's they say it was weather balloon testing against the Commies and the bodies were dummies. And people bought it!

You know all about these incidences if you're reading this, this isn't your first time knowing this, so I won't delve into every single detail about it. There are plenty of other books out there with these facts. But why? Why would the government want to cover this up? For our protection? Or to manipulate alien entities and be able to further control the masses of puppets in the world?

MJ12, Majestic 12, was the code name in 1947 of a group of scientist, military, leaders, and government officials and was formed by Executive order by then President Harry S. Truman. They wanted to recover and investigate alien spacecraft. No one really knew about this until 1984 when the papers were leaked but the Federal Bureau of Investigation shut them down as "bogus" and phonies".

Now I personally don't care much for Truman as a president mainly because his escalation of the Communist so-called threat to the world and his actions with Korea and Vietnam. But I do believe MJ12 existed because technology began to boom after this.

MJ12 supposedly is just fiction made up to make the government look bad. That's why they tell you. They say the documents are bogus, a conspiracy theory. But who funded this? Because it did exist. And Roswell was just one place, Between January 1947 and December 1952 at least 16 crashed or downed alien craft, 65 alien bodies, and 1 live alien were recovered. An additional alien craft had exploded, and nothing was recovered from that incident. Of these incidents, 13 occurred within the borders of the United States not including the craft which disintegrated in the air. Of these 13, 1 was in Arizona, 11 were in New Mexico, and 1 was in Nevada. Three occurred in foreign countries. Of those 1 was in Norway, and the last 2 were in Mexico. Sightings of UFO's were so numerous that serious investigation and debunking of each report became impossible utilizing the existing intelligence assets. MJ12 was funded by the military office of the USA, and it led to the creation of the National Security Agency by a secret order of the President on November 4, 1952. It led to the creation of several underground facilities that are top secret including Area 51.

Why won't the government tell us the truth? They condition us through books, movies, and magazines. Because it's about power and control. They don't want to lose control of the masses and the sheeple.

LISTEN TO THE MOCKINGBIRD

We are bombarded daily with media. Newspapers, television, internet, social media, billboards, you name it, it's out there and kind of straight out of the book 1984 by George Orwell. Orwell showed what happens when you re-write history and tell the people what you want them to believe, not the truth. And Orwell died at the young age of 47 supposedly of tuberculosis under the care of a young lady he dated or courted as they called it back then much to the concern of his friends. And that's what happens you speak out and think thoughts that "they" don't agree with.

But Orwell and many others opened the minds of many who realized they couldn't trust what they were being fed daily. Newspapers and books all have the agenda of the writer or company that pays for the writing. And it's worse today than it was back then.

In the early 1950's the U.S. Government, Central Intelligence Agency (CIA), started a covert operation called operation mockingbird which was, and probably still is, a domestic propaganda campaign aimed at promoting the views of the CIA within the media. Reporters shared their notebooks with the CIA. Editors shared their staffs.

CIA operatives were on the payroll of many media outlets planting false stories in the press. Because back then all people had was radio and newspapers, because television was just starting to get big. The CIA denied this until it became exposed in the 70's in Senate hearings. The hearings were about whether the CIA had too much power!

Now, in the days of today and mass media, we are hammered to no end and exposed at every turn to multimedia. We share our travels, our check ins, our bank accounts, and personal information, all online. Our lives are on the grid. Have a cell phone? They're tracking you! And we make it easier than ever. Alexa, Google home, spy on me please!

Orwell wrote of the tele speak, a device which beamed news into your home and could watch your every move. Now with the television, if they can beam something into your home what makes you think they can't beam things out of your home? Every home has one, on average 96% of every American household has a television, according to

Nielsen, the ratings people. They estimate there are over 285 million televisions in the USA! Think about that. How else can you control the masses? Media!

They tell you what to buy, what to wear, how to think, who to hate. Our media today is the most obvious biased media, and it seems to be worse than state-controlled media. They give you the perception that you are doing your own thinking but you're just being programmed by them all. They don't care about you. Just ratings and money.

Wake up people! Unplug, think for yourselves. The internet is full of websites that everyone is always quoting. Encyclopedias have been replaced by Wikipedia, which is wrote by, not experts, but the average person. It's not gospel. Even that's been changed over the years.

The truth lays in wait to be found. With some time and research, it's there. Wikipedia is fakeipedia and it's just more of the lies they want you to believe. Snopes is paid for by its advertisers, you think someone is going to cross them. They've hired a woman who they used to attack in their own articles as a liar. They have an agenda. Almost everyone has an agenda to make you believe and think their way because they feel their way is the only way, the right way. NO! It's not. Remove the blinders because they're lying to you. You can ask "well, what's your agenda?" My agenda is to help you, to get you to think on your own again, stop believing the lies and hatred. Use your brain, common sense, it can't be dead. Come together instead of drifting further apart!

Mockingbird exist today just under another name. The CIA, NSA, FBI, all run their covert operations, just in different areas under different names. Don't feel that you are being watched all the time though, they don't have enough people on their payroll for that. That's why they depend on others to turn people in. And if they were so great why do so many bad things happen to America? Monitoring everything, still didn't see 9/11 coming. No, because they were behind it!

False Flags

In the days of privateers and pirates they would fly a countries flag at sea and when they'd come across a ship that ship would be comfortable to see the Union Jack or Spanish Flag, until the flag came down and up went a pirate flag. Then they would attack after deceiving the other ships and causing them to put their guard down. It became to be known as a false flag.

Today, false flags refer to a covert operation designed to deceive, and it is designed to create the appearance of a party, group, or country to make them look responsible for some activity, while disguising the true actual source of responsibility. This is nothing new. It's been happening for years all over the world.

The American government has been running false flags for years, like the infamous Gulf of Tonkin incident to get the USA involved even more in Vietnam. In case you don't know the Gulf of Tonkin was an incident where a Vietnamese ship fired at a US ship, so we had the right to fire back and declare war. Many said that incident never happened, including people on the very ship itself. But you need a reason for war, not a good one, just a patriotic one people will believe in even it's a flat out lie.

Many people feel 9/11 was a false flag especially with the collapse of tower 7 which looks more like a controlled demolition than most controlled demolitions look! Gas attacks, bombs through the mail, mass shootings. Heck, we still don't know much about the Vegas shooting from 2017. No video of a man hauling a huge load of guns & ammo in a Vegas hotel. No witnesses? Seriously?

Countries have been doing this for years to get people riled up, to hate others, to separate and divide, to get a call to go to war. The Russians did it in 1939 as a basis to go to war against Finland, Japan has done it in 1931 to justify an invasion of Manchuria. The Nazis did it in 1933 as they burned down the Parliament building and blamed it on the Communist to stir up hatred leading the Nazis to control power. You can go back throughout time and governments and leaders always do this. Because they could care less about the people, it's all about control of the people and getting them to believe their lies.

Some of the leaders/countries have even admitted to doing this. No big deal to them. Who is going to punish them? You see protestors and counter protestors? Most of the time they are paid and many times they are undercover agents or police officers. This has been proven many times when someone talks or gets caught. Television shows even do it for ratings, they get caught, maybe pay a fine, and then work harder to not get caught. You and I lie we go to prison.

The Arab Spring was a movement that originated in Tunisia in December 2010 and quickly took hold in Egypt, Libya, Syria, Yemen, Bahrain, Saudi Arabia, and Jordan. It was supposedly because of oppressive regimes and low standards of living, which makes sense. But who created these uprisings? Who helped arm these people with no money? After all, you would see many of them in the streets with some nice weaponry. The US government under President Barack Obama poured billions of dollars into foreign military programs and supposed anti-terrorism campaigns to overtake these Middle Eastern authoritarian governments. Billions of American taxpayers' money. But it wasn't to stop terrorism, it was to help put their people in charge under the guise of terrorism because if the truth were told the American people would not buy into it. A classic false flag!

And what happened? The US set up leaders over in those countries who were even worse than the prior ones before them. But if they do what the US ask at that time it was seemingly ok. They didn't care about the people over there. Many of the real protestors, the young, ended up mysteriously "vanishing." But the media puts a positive spin on it, Obama listened to his puppet masters and says what he is told to say, and the people believed the lies!

After 9/11 how much of the USA was eager to go to war and invade Iraq? The Iraq resolution authorized the use of military force against Iraq in 2002 because of 9/11. It passed in the House by more than a 2-1 margin and in the Senate by more than a 3-1 margin. The justification was somehow Iraq was behind 9/11 and refused weapons of mass destruction inspections by the United Nations. So, the US went to war which caused over 4,000 young people to lose their lives and another 40,000 to be wounded. Those are US forces only, no one is exactly sure how many Iraqis died. And somehow this gave us a clear path to invade Afghanistan. Just like Vietnam, bombing innocent people and killing them in the name of what someone else thinks it's right for them.

Now right away from day one the US media and government declared that Osama Bin Laden carried out these attacks, that he was the mastermind behind it, although Saudis were flying the planes. The US government even flew Bin Laden's family out of the country for their safety? What?? Are you kidding me???

But there was no actual proof other than some doctored videos and sound bytes that came out from him now and then which when they did come out, it seemed that man in his early 50's got younger and younger.

Afghanistan is recorded as the longest war in US history, 2001 until the present, even though most of the job of defeating the Taliban was taken care of in the first year, but troops were left there to fight "insurgents". We invaded there under the guise of finding Osama Bin Laden, the 6 feet, five-inch Arab who walked with a cane and had to have dialysis because of kidney problems. Now, he should have been easy to find, even hiding in the caves. Was he the mastermind behind 9/11? Maybe. We will never know because he was supposedly found by Seal Team 6 hiding in a mansion in Pakistan. They stormed the compound (illegally mind you, not allowed in Pakistan without their government's permission) using drones and killed him. He was wrapped in a carpet and buried at sea from the USS Carl Vinson ship. They said they did it within 24 hours to observe Islamic tradition. He was supposedly identified by DNA test to conclude it was really him. But the pictures I saw of this prove nothing. There were no weapons in the pictures. (Yes, I have connections.) Why shoot an unarmed man sleeping if he is the most wanted terrorist in the world? And drop him in the middle of the Ocean? The US said no country would accept his remains but as a martyr for his people, an Islamic nation probably would have accepted him, including Pakistan who was quite angry that this went down in their country with no approval or knowledge of it, no matter what the media tries to say.

How would you feel if someone came into your neighborhood from another country and killed your neighbors in the middle of the night? I doubt you would like that; I know I wouldn't. I'd feel a bit violated and scared that there is no protection. Oh, and how would you feel if there were kids present, young kids to watch all this go down?

Now many people have filed Freedom of Information Acts (FOIA) and have all been denied? Hmmmm, I wonder why? Is there something to hide? Is someone lying?

Now under Islamic law burial at sea is only okay if no other burial purposes are available. The Sunni Muslims say in their learning that this a huge affront to their religious and human values. You think Obama would know, that right? But the US said they didn't want his grave or compound to be a shrine. The compound has been razed and an amusement park is planned for its place. But in the Muslim/Islamic religion people are not allowed to worship shrines. To me, and it should be obvious to you, we were lied to. Bin Laden was probably killed in the bombings of Afghanistan in 2002. But they had to do this to make the US look good and Obama look good. The real kicker of this? Sadly, 22 of the men from Seal Team 6 on that raid died in a helicopter crash thus stirring up more speculation. Coincidence? No! Coverup!

Now I'm not knocking the US military or anyone in that capacity because without them our country would not have the freedoms still that we have. I couldn't write this in most countries. Like most countries, many military members disagree with the regime and things they are told but still must follow orders and the chain of command.

Another great false flag operation was the Lusitania, a great ship carrying lots of cheese and butter. But it wasn't. It was struck by a German U Boat torpedo and exploded because of the munitions it was carrying illegally on it. 5 days before it was sunk the US ambassador to England

Walter Hines Page wrote a letter to his son stating that "if a British passenger ship carrying Americans is blown up, what will Uncle Sam do? That's what's going to happen."

And that's what happened. 1,100 people died including 120 Americans and that is what the United States needed to go to war. They needed an excuse.

Growing up I never believed our country could do such things. How could we sacrifice our own people to justify actions? It's horrible to think anybody, any entity, any government could do such things. We don't want to believe it, so we look away and hope it isn't true. But that's what they want you to do, accept the lies and look away with blind patriotism.

And one more great yet horrific example is that of President Franklin Delano Roosevelt (FDR) moving the US into World War 2. It was right after the great depression and there were no jobs to be found so FDR spent millions of dollars we didn't have to try to create jobs for his "New Deal." Now many good things did come out of it but most of it got the US further in debt. At this time, the US was staying out of WW2 because the consensus of the people of the nation was to stay out of it, despite knowing all the atrocities and hate filled evil things the Germans, Nazis, were doing to the Jews and other people they had no use for.

But FDR knew the only way to turn the country around was to get involved in the war. After all, war is big money for big business plus it takes out a bit of the surplus population. So, FDR arranged to have the US Naval Fleet to be relocated from San Pedro, off the coast of California, to Pearl Harbor, unprotected in the middle of the Pacific. This incensed Admiral James Richardson, the commander in chief of the US fleet. He bitterly complained about this action since it was 2,000 miles from US mainland and left the fleet open to attack from every direction. It also cut down on the supply chain and packed all the ships closely together, sitting ducks per se for an easy attack. FDR did this anyway and relieved Richardson of his command!

In June of 1941 US Secretary of the Interior Harold Ickes pushed FDR into putting an embargo on the oil supplied to the Japanese. 3 weeks later all Japanese assets were frozen. For no real justifiable reason. 4/5 of the oil imported for Japan came from America so this shut down their economy.

Now the US listened on the Japanese military broadcast, the Honolulu paper predicted an attack was imminent, and the carriers were dispatched to sea. There were so many warnings that an attack was coming, and the US and FDR knew it! Even to this day documents surface proving this.

In November of 1941 FDR stated that "the United States desires Japan commits the first overt act". And they did!

On December 7, 1941, Pearl Harbor was attacked by the Japanese and killed over 2,400 Americans in a "sneak attack". FDR got his wish because Americans rallied around the flag and were now ready for war. They took all Japanese citizens and locked them up in camps across the US.

Never mind most were innocent of everything except being born Japanese. This executive order by FDR was even upheld by the US Supreme court. Never mind the fact that Jews were being brutally slaughtered over in Germany, but America didn't care until it affected them directly. Much like today, even back then people were selfish with little empathy.

You're being lied to people. You're being used to hate, separate, divide. Divide and rule, oldest trick in the book going way back to this saying being accredited to the Greek Phillip II of Macedon. Julius Caesar used this, Flavius Josephus wrote of this, it's been around forever, and it's easily done especially now in the 21st century.

THE SOCIAL MEDIA CONTROL

In 1971 the first electronic mail (email) was sent by computer engineer Ray Tomlinson. It was simply a test message to himself. The email was sent from one computer to another computer sitting right beside it in Cambridge, Massachusetts, but it traveled via ARPANET, a network of computers that was the precursor to the Internet.

Now the internet, (interacted network contraction) goes back to the 1960's when, surprise, surprise, the US government was trying to build fault free untraceable connections from one computer to another. This evolved into the commercial rise of the internet starting into the 90's and evolving into what we have today. Instant secure access to anything at your fingertips.

But is it secure? Is it safe? Or like in the great book by George Orwell, 1984, is Big Brother just all connecting us to make us easily controlled? You look at your main search engines, your social media pages, they're all controlled. And so, are you.

Search something, you'll only find what they want you to find. You need to dig deep for the truth, but they will hide that, bury that. Think I'm lying or crazy? Try it, you know it's true. Search for something in Amazon, then you'll get an ad for what you searched on Facebook. But you're ok with that if you get your package and can troll the web.

People walk around with their face to their phone, can't communicate because they can only do it through text, have extraordinarily little life skills at all! Palm people I call them. They know where you are always, where you like to go, what you like to eat. They don't need to tap the phones anymore you're giving them all they need to know for free! You're making their job easy for them.

I still remember the day when I realized technology had gone too far, had gotten too advanced. It was in 1996 when Deep Blue, an IBM computer, played genius chess master Gary Kasparov in chess. It beat him in the first game, but he won the rest. So, it was "heavily redesigned and upgraded" and the computer beat him. He walked away from the table, and I'll never forget the look on his face as if he knew the world we knew would be no more. For some reason that always stuck with me.

People play so called freemium games, which start out free but get you to spend money because getting more and more release that dopamine in your brain. Getting more and more likes is like smoking crack. These game companies, app companies, they know this. Heck, it's the same things casinos have been doing for years. They use red to stimulate the brain more, flashing lights and sounds, they get you excited to keep you gaming. They spend lots of money to figure these things out. It's not about making you happy, it's about making them money! Interesting side note for Christians here, did you know all the numbers of a roulette wheel added up equals to 666? Weird, Huh?

As we glide into the future, we must realize that we are so dependent on the internet and computers if the grid goes down, we are all screwed! And that's what they want to do to control you and be your masters even more than they are now. It will be China under Mao, people killing and eating their own children, or even under Venezuela right now where the people have nothing despite living in an oil rich nation, where they are forced to stay alive by eating garbage or their pets.

DRUGS R BAD M'MKAY

Another form of control over the masses is to keep them doped up with, well, actual dope. Drugs are big business. They've been bringing them up here for years. Sure, we hear of the big bust now and then but how much gets through? Then they bust a big-time dope dealer he gets a little prison or none because he starts to work for the Feds. It's been proven on many occasions that our own government and that of other countries allow the drugs to come in with kickbacks and back-room arrangements.

In the 1980's our Central Intelligence Agency was importing drugs, Cocaine, into America and giving the profits to the Contras to help fight the war in Nicaragua. There was a huge investigation which cost taxpayers millions, yet nothing came of it.

You see, the US backed the Contras and we sold weapons to Iran and took the profits and gave it to the Contras to help support them. And when that was found out then came the Cocaine.

What? We sold weapons to Iran. The country that hates us, hates Israel, and would like nothing more to blow Israel off the planet, their exact words not mine. How deep does the rabbit hole go and where are the morals and values? Bob Dylan even said, "but to live outside the law you must be honest."

The war on drugs is a joke people. It really could be stopped but they don't want it to be. In the early 1970's Harlem drug kingpin Frank, "Superfly" Lucas was a huge heroin dealer. He brought the drug in from Southeast Asia smuggled in the coffins of dead American soldiers' coffins.

His heroin, blue magic, was everywhere. The movie American Gangster is based on his story.

Now why bring him up? Because he was moving hundreds of kilos (2.2 pounds) of dope a day. He's just one man. I'm sure there were lots of payoffs, rip-offs, look the other way along the way. He was just one man in one city with an ingenious idea. How many more are like him?

Sadly, most of the addicts are in the black communities, or your lower income areas, usually associated with black communities because of whiteouts and red lining, I'll be hitting that up later. And the same time the CIA was bringing in lots of cocaine was the exact same time crack was introduced to the black communities.

Drugs and alcohol are meant to control and keep people down. No longer does the Ku Klux Klan have to wear the white robes and hoods, racism comes in many forms. Ever wonder why there is a liquor store on every corner in a black neighborhood? Ever wonder why the police only get the small dealers and users off the streets? Because of systematic controlled racism. That's why they put crack in the black communities, that's why they support the division of gangs like the Crips and the Bloods. They will sell cocaine and weapons to them both, hoping they will kill one another. They don't care! And when white people get caught up in it, well, they don't need those people to fit the plan of their population control.

You know who the worst dope dealers around though? Big Pharmaceutical companies! And they're nice and legal. The US Food and Drug Administration

(FDA) has been around since 1906. Now my first thought is how are foods related to drugs. Two separate things, right? No, because they put synthetic drugs, toxic chemicals into our food and beverages.

Now, the FDA states it is responsible for protecting and promoting public health through the control and supervision of food safety, tobacco products, dietary supplements, prescription and over the counter drugs and medications, vaccines, biopharmaceuticals, blood transfusions, medical devices, electromagnetic radiation emitting devices (ERED), cosmetics, animal foods and feed, and veterinary products. That's a whole lot of stuff especially when a lot of it technically is not related to food or drugs.

But they are the ones who test things, approve it for the people. They decide what is safe for consumption. Like sugar substitutes. Whenever you see something taking the place of sugar, odds are what replaces it is even worse for you but just cheaper to manufacture because we don't want to cut into companies' profits and stockholders.

Like they did with saccharin. Remember saccharin from the 70's? It caused cancer in lab mice! Apparently, they didn't test it exceedingly long and approved it. In 1981 it was banned because it caused bladder cancer but for some reason in 2001 the warning labels were removed and it's okay now because their studies show the bladder cancer in the mice was not relevant to humans. Did you get that? Their study!

High Fructose corn syrup, another great substitute. Cheaper and easier to produce than sugar yet it causes colon cancer in lab mice, and it makes you fat! Extra weight leads to poor health. And to top it off it is usually produced with genetically modified (GMO) corn.

I could go on and on about the toxic crap put in our foods. Read the labels. If it has 20 letters in it, odds are it's a chemical not good for our bodies. Preservatives are horrible things. And don't be fooled by all natural or organic because the FDA allows many toxic cancer-causing chemicals to be certified as such. One of the worst is Xanthan Gum.

Xanthan Gum seemed to appear out of nowhere when many people started to try to eat better, which is hard for most families since the crap that will kill you food is cheap and good for you stuff is jacked up high on their prices. It is a thickening agent discovered in a lab and approved in the late 60's. It is a sucralose/glucose mix and is used besides in foods as an artificial sweetener, wallpaper glue, and in cosmetics. It is a chemical which does not digest in your body! This is a proven fact. Your liver can not filter it out. Why? Why is this allowed? Because of greed!!

They don't care about you or me. They only care about our money. They don't care if we die. Look at the US tobacco industry, they lose almost half a million of their loyal customers a year. But they keep producing their product knowing it will kill, knowing the side effects. I feel bad for the 41,000 people who die of secondhand smoke. But they don't care.

They come out with camel joe and marketing gimmicks like points and rewards, and you get a shirt or jacket for it. Or you used to. That's great, it looks good on you in your coffin!

Big Pharma is destroying our world. They control the drugs, the prices, the suppliers, the pharmacies, and more. Lobbyists spend millions for them to get their drugs as the main ones used. They produce addictive drugs which are pushed by some overly prescription happy doctors controlled by Big Pharm to keep you under control. Not all doctors are like that. Nor are all hospitals. Many care and will get to the root of the problem and fix you. I call them healers. Most of the things that are overly medicated such as attention deficit disorder (ADD), and other diseases requiring medication which usually keep you as a customer.

But if you go online to see a report, you'll get mixed reviews. Let me just tell you, people get paid for reviews, the big industries will spend millions to trick you and deceive you. Harry Truman said it best, "if you can't convince them, confuse them!"

KEEPING "DARKY" DOWN

Yes, the title of the chapter sounds harsh but sadly it's true. In 1654 in what would later become the United States of America a Mr. John Casor became the first indentured servant to be declared a slave in a civil case in Virginia. Slavery was legal in all 13 original colonies and was legal until the 13th amendment in 1863 when still half the states then still allowed slavery. Because even though President Abraham Lincoln signed the Emancipation Proclamation, the so-called slave states had seceded and were no longer part of the United States, so they didn't have to follow that order. Don't be fooled either and manipulated by false history, the Northern states were just as guilty as the South. As a matter of fact, many of the ports where most slaves were entering into the United States from Africa were in the Northern States. Many of the so-called free states had laws on their books to keep freed or escaped slaves from owning property or even truly being freed. They couldn't vote. Laws were set up to keep them from getting jobs. Several Northern states would send slaves back to their owners for cash rewards.

A caste system was born out of all this as people took advantage of freed Black people after 1865. Not only were they looked down upon by color but by the fact they were poor.

When the slaves were freed, they had nowhere to go. No money, no property, no transportation. Nothing! That was when the sharecropping took place. They were given land to farm & shacks to live in but had to share the crops and profits in exchange for rent. In a way, although free, black people were still slaves. Kept down by greedy, richer people who knew how to take advantage of others and how to keep people down.

Segregation was still real. Separate but not even close to being treated as equal. And of course, they were kept down by laws made to keep black people down, by the Southern Democrats. They couldn't own guns, land, couldn't go to schools, and of course although given the right to vote in 1870, laws were attached to that so they couldn't vote. They were basically still enslaved.

And if they had a rough year with the crops many would face eviction or must go into debt until they could pay the landowner.

Now not everyone was like this. Some people cared about others much like today. Good people that fought hard and gave their lives. People like white abolitionist John Brown. There are good people everywhere in every generation. But for the vast majority at the time, the black people were blamed for the War between the states and were treated like dirt. Many made their way back to Africa, in Liberia for example, thanks to the American Colonization Society (ACS) who believed black people would be better off in Africa than in America.

But over the years and even to this day many people have done horrible things to the black people in the USA and have worked hard to keep them down. They have forced them into low-income areas and do whatever it takes to keep them there. The laws of segregation were finally lifted in 1954 when black people could attend schools with whites at the state level. In 1964, the Civil Rights Act superseded all state and local laws against segregation. But it still wasn't enough.

Many great men gave their lives to make people open their eyes and realize although different color we are equal, humans. Even though segregation was outlawed it still existed. And to this day it still exists in many ways, they just don't call it that and they don't say what they are doing. The Whites Only signs are gone but the sentiment is still there.

They now do it through the banking systems, through redlining, which is to deny a loan because they live in a poor area or are deemed to be a financial risk. I have known people with great credit scores who can't get a home loan because of things like this. They have institutionalized the racism in America. And they still want division.

When it comes to hiring who are they going to call in for an interview, Jamal, or Keith? Tamika or Karen? I've seen it firsthand; I have heard it firsthand. And when a black man or woman is hired in a predominantly white environment, they still have problems. People feel like they're a slave. Any person that feels that way obviously is being treated that way and it's not just in their mind. It's sad and should not be happening in our society.

Back in the late 60's especially you had the "white outs" or "white flight" where the white people moved out of urban areas. Then the suburban areas jacked up all the rents and housing cost. And it was to keep black people and so-called poor people out of their communities. And it's even worse today.

In my city an average house goes for $45,000 and that's a nice neighborhood. In the suburbs? $355,000 according to Zillow! That's no lie. And that's not a mansion with lots of property. And you think the playing field is fair and equal?

They don't need the Ku Klux Klan anymore. Now they keep Black people down as much as possible with movies, music, computers, and mass media.

They portray and stereotype black people in movies as gangsters, drug addicts, hookers, thieves, and as stupid. And other races see this and believe it. The music is negative, degrading to women and others. And other black people are behind a lot of this.

Yes, I'm saying black people. I grew up when it was colored, then negro, then black, then in the mid 80's it became African-American. But all my friends and family say black. So, don't get offended, the world is too easily offended anyway.

Yes, black people have made great strides but when you get told by society you can't get ahead unless you play up to the stereotypes and you are kept down it's hard to believe you can get ahead. And one of the worst racist to black people? Other black people.

If a black person succeeds, they are called sellout, uncle tom, a slave. But it's all part of a horrible system that's designed to keep people down. And then you have white people that can quote every statistic as far as black on black crime goes or black people having opportunity, yet they live in an all-white environment, and they don't have any black friends. Well, they will say they have a black friend and that's always one of the most racist things you'll ever hear. I know a guy who drops the N word like nothing, and he has 4 biracial grandkids. This is a big part of the problem. They want black people held down; they don't want them to get ahead. Oh, sure they'll say it, but they don't mean it. To me action means more than words and I see negative action when it comes to keeping the black community down.

You have so called civil right leaders, basically pimps wearing three-piece suits saying they care for black people, but they are nothing but snake oil salesman trying to keep you under their control and keep racism alive for profit, theirs not yours. You know who I mean, millionaires who don't live in the ghetto. Oh, sure they may have seen some racism in their day but not anymore in their mansions in gated communities. They eat dinners that cost more than some families earn in a week. They dine with the high and mighty, drive fancy cars, go everywhere in limos. Yet they claim they represent you?

Liquor stores on every corner (which are never owned by black folks let alone locally owned), promoting gang violence while the police look away, mistrust placed in the police for many proper reasons, introducing crack to the black neighborhoods and other drugs. It's how they keep Black people down and addicted to poverty. It's all part of their evil plan. And yes, crack did not just come out of nowhere like the Internet wants you to believe that it was made affordable to make the drug dealers richer who were losing money. The drug dealers are billionaires living in foreign nations bringing the stuff into our country and our government brought crack into the black community to keep black people addicted to drugs and to keep them down. Because they don't care because racism is still rampant in America.

As I write this we are amid a global pandemic and an even uglier pandemic which is racism. The Black Lives Matter movement is opening the eyes of people everywhere but at the same time dividing the US of A because many people don't care about black people. Plain and simple. Many are protesting in support but only when the weather is nice and only in their all-white communities which are designed to keep minorities out. They say black lives matter, but they don't want them in their neighborhoods. They don't march or anything when it's cold or snowing so I guess to them black lives matter when its trending to make them look and feel good about themselves. It's almost like black lives matter except when the weather is bad or when they have something better to do. Also, I see many people holding signs in all white communities or putting a sign up in an all-white community, a community that is designed to keep minorities out by keeping the rents high. They are a big part of the problem. How can you March for black people when you don't know any or have any in your community? They only care when it can make them look good and they must get pictures to brag about what they do. Kind of like when they give a dollar to homeless man, they can't do a good deed unless everyone knows it and it makes them look good.

They say, "I'm not a racist I work with a black guy, or I hired one." No, they're racist. If they really cared they'd go into a black community and help clean up trash, invest in the area to create jobs, volunteer at homeless shelters and soup kitchens, but they don't. Because many only pay lip service.

The politicians? The ones elected year after year to help with communities, all communities in their districts. They only care about black people when it's time to get that vote. Oh, sure many big city downtown areas look nice but leave and go where most people must live. Think about this, Detroit is the highest percentage city for black people with an 83% African American population. It's also the city with the highest poverty rate. Is that because black people want to be poor or because they can't handle money very well? Or is it because they are kept down by systemic racism? What do you think?

These power-hungry people at the top never wanted slaves to be free. There are many quotes, too many to list here, by wealthy people who wanted to send them back to Africa. Instead, let's just keep them down. That is what they want. Let's divide races, poor whites, you got more than the Black people don't complain. It's all by design.

Now I keep saying they and you want to know who they are. Keep reading because the rabbit hole is deep, and it will blow your mind.

BLAME IT ON THE JEWS

The Hebrews, the Jews, have been documented throughout world history since almost 5,800 years. Much is known of their great history, and they have brought forth great things to our modern society such as inventions, medical breakthroughs, cures for diseases, literacy, laws of justice, rights for women, value of all human life, equality, and much more.

They have produced good environmentally energy sources, such as solar and drip irrigation. They've made great strides in chemistry, physics, mathematics, and economics. Yet for everything positive they've done for all mankind they are probably the most hated group of people on the planet Earth. More hate crimes are committed against Jewish people yearly not just in America but throughout the world. According to the FBI crime statistics on hate crimes, Jewish people made up about 75% of the hate crimes in America in 2021 yet make up only about 2% of the population. Most people don't care because empathy and compassion are a thing of the past for many, and they don't care because they're not Jewish. People only seem to care about something when it pertains or affects them directly. Or if it's trendy for them to make then look good and feel good about themselves and in the eyes of others.

Yes Jewish, Judaism is a religion, but it is also a race passed down proudly through the mother's bloodline, some different religious groups of Judaism will say it's ok to be passed down through the father's bloodline also. Yet since the dawn of documented creation the Jews have been enslaved many times, killed, ran off their own land which their Creator gave them, faced a huge diaspora which spread them all over Europe only to be persecuted even more, kicked out of countries like Spain, and we all are aware of what happened to the Jews in the 30's & 40's. Yet why? Well, the Jews ask themselves that question to this very day as they are still heavily persecuted. Even as I write this there were attacks on Jewish people today for no reason than other than being a Jew! In New York City and around the world they are trying to blame Covid19 on the Jewish community. Famous people speak out against the Jews and try to use their influence to get people to believe their points of views. It's like 1930' s Germany all over again.

The Jews are the most persecuted people on the planet. They make up .2% of the human population yet anti-Semitic attacks are up over 19,000%! There are only 14 million Jews in the world and there are people that have more followers than that on Instagram and Facebook. Imagine being in a select small group of people and being persecuted for nothing more than being who and what you are.

The Jew brought forth Christianity which evolved out of their own religion and other religions too. Yet they too, mostly, hate the Jew. Oh, they say they support them but saying something and doing something are two different things. When the time comes who stands with Israel and the Jew? The Christian will look away because they don't want to be persecuted. Plus, they still have in their mind the myth that the Jews killed Jesus.

Hollywood, television, music, the internet, books, anti-Semitism is everywhere and somehow it seems to be a bit socially acceptable. Why? Who is behind it? I mean you just don't wake up and hate a race for no reason, it's a learned behavior.

You hear the stories of the Jew, the stereotype of a big nosed money-grubbing greedy backstabber. The book Protocols of Zion came out in Russia in the late 19th century, and were proven to be a falsehood, and it stirred up the masses to hate the Jews. They've been blamed for everything from the Christian Jesus' death to 9/11! Hitler used them to get his Nazi cause going. And other governments knew that, knew what he was doing including the American president FDR and the USA itself, but they all turned a blind eye. But why?

Since the dawn of Judaism, the Jews have been persecuted. Since day 1. Everyone is out to get them. Why? What did they ever do wrong? Besides the lies people tell. Why would less than 1% of the world be the most persecuted population since there have been records kept and written word? To this day, all you see in the news is antisemitism daily. Countries want to wipe them out. They have the land mass the size of the US' Connecticut, not very much. And it is and was their land until they got run off it. That land and more is theirs. History has proven it. They have had medical breakthroughs like no other and are a very advanced country. They don't attack, they defend. Yet people, not all but many, just want them gone.

What does anyone have to gain from hatred of the Jews? Why would they promote this? Who would support this?

The answer is coming up and you might not like it, but it is the straight truth, 100% factual. The truth is stranger than fiction!

BORN AGAIN

There are over 4,000 major religions in our world. There are even more when you consider minor sects that are not affiliated with the major religions. And then there are practices that are not considered religions, but that people follow to achieve enlightenment and to maybe get a better afterlife.

The three major religions are Christianity with about 1/3 of the world practicing that, about 2 billion people. There are many different forms of Christianity including Catholics, Protestant, Mormons, Jehovah's Witnesses, and more. Although different with their teachings they all believe in the gospel and belief that Jesus Christ is the Messiah as prophesied in their Bible. Many have different books they practice from, but the Holy Bible

(Latin for good book) is their main book for most of them.

Next largest is Islam, with over 20% of the world practicing it, about 1.8 billon people. They believe there is only one God (monotheistic), and that Muhammad is the true messenger or prophet.

Both these religions surprisingly are derived from the Hebrew religion Judaism. They find their roots in the Torah, the books of Moses, or first five books of the Bible. And the Tanakh, the rest of the old Jewish books which Christians call the Old Testament.

Islam however believes a bit different getting their roots from Abraham and they have derived it from there. Most historians believe that Islam originated in Mecca and Medina about the 7th century CE (common era) about 600 years after the beginning of Christianity. Christianity started in 1 CE after Jesus died, but it did not gain in popularity until much later. Many of the scriptures of what is referred to as the New Testament were wrote many years after Jesus died and many by people who did not even know him in his lifetime.

The third largest religion with about a billion followers is Hinduism. Hinduism is the practice of Dharma, or way of life and is considered the oldest religion of the world. Many scholars refer to it as the eternal way. It is a remarkably diverse religion with no governing body, or prophets. Its purpose is to connect with life, nonviolence, rebirth, and it's hard to define it as a strict religion.

Why am I bringing up religions? Because there are so many and when you are born, most, not all, but most people are taught, or indoctrinated I should say, to believe a certain way, usually the ways of their families. And if you disagree, or stray, you are considered a heathen, a sinner, or in some cases, you get put to death. You are what you are taught unless you grow up to explore other ideas on your own. And when you question things, you become the outcast or the bad guy.

What makes one religion right but not another? What religion is the best one, the right one? Who is to say? People fight wars in the name of their gods or religions. They give their lives in the name of their religions. And they cast you aside if you disagree with them.

Most people have never read the Bible or Koran. They quote verses but they never really read it or studied it. And they took the Hebrew writings and translated it to their own way, thus distorting the message. They practice what they want and blow off many of G-ds rules because it doesn't really apply anymore because they were old and so long ago and times have changed, or they will dismiss it and say it's only for the Jews who G-d was talking to then. Yet they will take other rules, in the same book, same chapter and practice those. They will judge you for many things even though their Jesus said not to. They will say they support Israel because their Jesus was Jewish but won't honor the laws of Torah or holidays like Jesus did, because he was Jewish! And why? Because people are fickle and hypocrites!

You are raised in a religious home, you are taught that, you must believe it, because it's the only way. I see so many

Christians attacking other faiths or even sects of their own Christianity branches because it's not their way, and in their minds their way is the only way. It's kind of like that with anything. You are indoctrinated at a young age, usually since birth, to believe a certain way. Whether it's sports teams, religion, or politics. Sports teams are not such a bad thing, but religion and politics are!

They tell you to use Blind Faith. And that's okay. It's ok to have strong convictions about what you believe in, but you can't judge others for it. It's in the New Testament. It's clear. If you believe that. But everything you are taught is not always right. It is not always the way because you say it is. Misinterpretations come into play quite a bit and so does harsh judgment.

And to top it off, most religions are a big business!! Religion in the USA is worth over $1.5 trillion a year. If it were its own country, it would be the 15th largest economy in the world. And they don't have to pay taxes in the United States!! Christians, the religion, hold over half the world's wealth. Now why if something is good and enlightening to others do you have to charge for it? Look at all these mega churches popping up all over America. They say it's to spread the word of G-d, but is it? You have preachers getting rich, living in million-dollar homes, and walking past the homeless and poor to get to their churches. You could sell a stained-glass window in a church and feed a poor family for a year.

Religion is in many ways a good thing because it helps people deal with the unanswered questions of the universe. It helps them feel better about why we are here and what happens in the afterlife. It can give people a sense of purpose and calmness, a sense of peace and understanding. And that's a good thing. But you must practice what you preach and let others that disagree with you believe their way too. Everyone has a different purpose and different way to enlightenment. Don't question their way or judge them. Don't think your religion is the only way. Remember to live and let live. And think freely and let others do the same.

OH, NOOOOO IT'S MR. BILL

Remember Saturday Night Live back in the day when it used to be funny and entertaining? They had a character made from clay called Mr. Bill which would get into all kinds of bad situations thanks to Mr. Hands and Sluggo. As I travelled this country, I met a real-life Mr. Bill who had problems too. Only his were caused by an evil government regime who wanted him gone because he knew too much.

You'll meet many people in this world that will tell you stories of things they have encountered. Some are fabrications stretched to get attention, but many times the things you learn and hear which are the most farfetched are the ones that true. As always, truth can be stranger than fiction.

I have traveled all over this country for many years and other countries and have met many interesting people along the way. Some will be standing on a street corner telling a story while people just walk by them and ignore them but sometimes the stories, they're telling are a bit intriguing and it makes you wonder if it's true. But people will write them off as a nut job because that's easy to do because again, the truth is stranger than fiction and people would rather live in a little sheltered world and not think that the government and corrupt powers would be out to hurt them and take advantage of them. I mean after all we're taught from day one that the government loves us and will take care of us and look after us.

So, I've met and talked to many interesting people and have sat down and had great conversations with them. Some of them are authors and have published books. Others just want to talk and tell the story and don't want everything in writing because they want to stay off the grid. They're completely off the grid and try to stay out of the limelight because they know what happens to people in the limelight that tell the truth. The truth against the powers that be.

I did not come from a privileged home. I left home at an early age, and I've had to work for everything I have. Nothing was ever handed to me. I worked for it or had to fight for it. It's been a struggle at times. I have lived in the ghettos, have slept in vehicles, slept outdoors, and have broken into abandoned buildings to get out of the rain. I've been up and I've been down. I've ate at soup kitchens and homeless shelters. I have seen people beaten and robbed; I've even seen people get killed. It's never been easy for me, but I don't complain because it's made me who I am today.

 But I've also sat down and ate and partied with multi-millionaires. I've made many connections throughout the years. I've met politicians, professional athletes, rock stars, actors, and actresses. I've met millionaire businessman and media moguls. I've stayed in penthouses and have been private parties full of the rich and famous at which I probably did not belong. And in all classes, there is good and bad people. The people I've met along the way some have really influenced me others I feel sorry for. And some, some changed my life forever.

Thus, my friend I met many years ago by happenstance, Mr. Bill. I met Mr. Bill (I'm not going to mention his real name for his protection) on the California coast way back when. He rolled into town one day and nobody knew where he came from or really who he was. But he started hanging out on the street with us and he had some interesting thoughts and points of view. He was just not another rambling street person who needed mental help or was strung out on drugs. There was something quite different about him I noticed right away.

Everyone considered him a wingnut, a whack job. The things he would say were extremely out there to most. But many of the things he had mentioned had already happened and were exposed and many things he had talked about that were going to happen did happen. So, I always wondered how he knew what was going down. He seemed very sincere and genuine and some of the things he would mention I had heard of in other circles of friends who were in the know. I got to know him quite well. It turns out he was a Harvard educated egghead who worked for the American Central Intelligence Agency (CIA) for many years but had to leave because he did something he believed immoral, but the CIA believed was for the good of the country and he lost it. He couldn't do what they wanted anymore. And the information and things he knew were amazing. Many things he talked about I saw unfold before my eyes, things that were planned out years in advance.

For instance, once he told me to stock up on ice and get a big cooler and get a propane heater and stock up on propane. I asked him why and he simply said, "trust me." I did. About a week later the grid for the whole area I was living in, a fairly large city and area, went down. No power for several days. The power grid had been attacked in an act of terrorism.

He knew quite a bit about thing before they happened. He was still in the know with many of his friends from the Agency. He would come up and say, "watch Iraq," then walk away. At the time nothing big was happening there. Most people had never heard of it. Next thing I knew, war. He could give you names of those involved before you'd ever heard of them.

He knew about the Iran-Contra scandal way before we even heard it on the news. When he brought it up it sounded like a major make-believe story, something out of the movies, with cocaine and funneling money to terrorist. But when it hit it sent a shiver down my spine knowing he saw it coming. Who predicts stuff like that? And he had all kind of stuff about President Bush the first. He was not a big fan. "Once CIA always CIA," Billy said.

We don't realize how controlled we are by these government agencies. They are not designed to protect us as much as they are designed to control us in the name of protection. They have a budget of ungodly proportions (FBI, CIA, NSA), and do they protect us? Or do they create wars, divide countries, take over countries to put leaders in power that America likes and controls?

Why did the CIA let Mr. Bill live since he knew so much? The man was a freaking genius and he predicted Bush senior would be president way before he even ran. He told me about the Gulf war way before anyone even dreamt of it. He predicted cell phones tracking us, the fake drug wars, shipping of weapons, rolling blackouts and power outages, cameras everywhere in the name of security even though it's to keep track of us, and more. Way too many things to list. He wasn't a prophet. He knew what was coming down because it's all been planned. These things are not spur of the moment things; they are put in place for a purpose. And they let him live because they figured people won't believe a "crazy" man. He was too obvious to be CIA, no one would believe him. But as I learned many years ago the best way to hide something is to put it in plain sight.

Speaking of CIA there have been many people in Mr. Bill's situation like most recently Edward Snowden. He became disillusioned with the unethical things he was involved with as a subcontractor with the CIA. And he blew the whistle. They painted him as a traitor, a liar, crazy, but the only real thing he did wrong to them was tell the truth. They charged him with espionage act of 1917. And of course, the USA/CIA won in court. They claim he hurt the country but all he did was expose the things being done wrong in the name and expense to the United States citizens and taxpayers. He got in trouble for telling the truth!

The CIA's job description is to collect information, but we all know there is much going on. It runs deeper than most of us can imagine. These people, agencies, have too much power. And they want to control every aspect of the world and its citizens. They don't care about us. We could die tomorrow, they don't care. They control more than we even know.

And we just let them. We pay for it. America's gone wrong.

As far as Mr. Bill goes the last time I ever saw him was in Washington DC several few years ago and he was talking to an Asian man about Israel and explaining many of the things going on with them. He always was a strong supporter of Israel and he stated we needed to recognize Jerusalem as Israel's capital. After all Jerusalem has USA in it. It's a major connection to him. And without USA there is no Jerusalem and vice versa. Most passed him by as a nutjob. But he swore the American embassy in Israel would finally be moved to Jerusalem thus declaring it as its capital and America would then recognize it as such. People laughed.

On December 6, 2017, President Donald J. Trump formally recognized Jerusalem as the capital of Israel and stated that the American embassy would be moved from Tel Aviv to Jerusalem.

It's good to know Mr. Bill is still out there connected and preaching the truth, and I hope he always will be.

WHO AND WHY?

Who wants to control everyone? Why? And how could one entity, one group control the world. There's 7 and a half billion people in the world. Billion! That's a lot so how could a group of say 1,000 people control the world? Or even less.

In January 1920, the league of Nations was created as a group to help promote world peace. It was started after World War 1 following the Paris Peace Conference. Not everyone liked it though because to join you had to accept the treaty of Versailles and not every country did, especially the Germans. Surprisingly, despite Woodrow Wilson's push for it, the United States did not participate in the League of Nations. Many felt it was unconstitutional. All it pretty much did was settle land disputes with other countries. And people feared the power it could have, especially American isolationist.

Then in 1945 a new group was created in San Francisco, California. After World War 2, the United Nations was formed. Its aim was to maintain international peace and develop friendly relations amongst countries. The UN Charter has for its main purposes: peace and security, developing relations, fostering cooperation, to solve the world's problems.

But the UN has become a problem to the world. A bully organization to many smaller countries. Since the 1950's it's been smacked with rampant anti-Semitism, globalism accusations, corruption, and abuses of its power.

Many of the larger countries control the majority. And of course, that makes the smaller country members feel less. Plus, they have been pushing for One World Government. They have known about such thing's countries have done as sterilization and there is no outcry from the UN for it. Many governments noticed a rise in forced child prostitution since the UN because they send in NATO troops, and they take advantage of the poor.

There was also the huge oil for food program which allowed Iraq to sell oil on the world market in exchange for food and medical needs. The program was by President Bill Clinton's administration in 1995. However, the program was rampant with corruption and the local citizens the program was for went without.

UN aid workers were also responsible for a Cholera outbreak, but nothing happened, and the UN claims diplomatic immunity.

Is the UN needed? Who funds it? 22 percent is funded by the United States. Out of 193 countries/members the USA taxpayers pick up the biggest tab. That's why no one wants to be a part of it. Plus, one organization where people are appointed not elected telling us or trying to tell the world, how to live the way they want us to live.

The USA pays more than 10 billion dollars a year to the United Nations. Yet there is still poverty, shortages of necessities like housing and water, and kids dropping dead in the street. Why? Think about what that money could do if you just directly used it on your own to help underdeveloped countries.

So, there is a quick and easy example of how someone could control the world, one group. Because money just doesn't talk, it curses!

Another group many people don't hear much of is the Bilderbergers. They're a group of rich people that meet every year. Established in 1954 they are named after the Hotel they first met at. Their goal or aim was to prevent another World war. But was that really the goal? Isn't that what the United Nations was formed for? Now they say their agenda is to bolster a free market Western capitalism around the globe.

About 130 political and so-called experts from finance, labor, academia, and media are invited to take part in the meeting. Two thirds of the groups are from Europe and the rest from North America. The meetings are conducted under the Chatham House Rule where participants are free to use the information received but neither the identity nor affiliation of the speaker may be revealed.

But who are they and what do they really want? By people being there when they arrive in their limos, they are easily identifiable. But what is the real goal? As in most group's real agenda its mission is for a one world government. But they won't tell you that. They, like most groups, will try to convince you they are for your good. And many people believe it. And when you question it, you're a conspiracy theorist nutjob. That's how they try to throw off the hounds that are hunting them and getting close, use a deception to make everyone look at others as the bad people.

2020 PLANDEMIC

As I write this the USA is in the worst pandemic it's seen in over 100 years. And then throw an ugly election on top of that. You all know about the Wuhan flu, coronavirus, covid-19, whatever you want to call it. It came from China in a lab and is destroying our country even worse than the two- party system does!

Yes, the virus is real, I know many people who have had it and have died from it. People argue over how bad it is but good news everybody, they have come out with a vaccine super quick. And billionaires are backing it. Especially the ones that have no medical background at all, but I guess with enough money you can purchase any degree you want in America.

We just came off the vilest election since Nixon ran against JFK, who by the way stole that election and then turned against his masters and look what it got him.

The election of 2020 was so bad it had to be recounted and had runoffs in several states. Was the election stolen? Probably. But you can't prove it. Look at the winning sides candidate. He's a bumbling idiot with obvious dementia factors who in his 40 plus years of politics has voted by party lines and the only bill he sponsored was to give minorities more prison time. Yet he got elected? Because his vice president nominee is a person of color and people want to feel good and say they made history.

That's what got Obama elected, white guilt. Diet racist, closet racist, say "oh look at me I voted for a negro, I'm not a racist." But they live in all white communities designed to keep minorities out with their high housing cost. One or two black families move in, it's ok, when several do property values drop and for sale signs go up. It's the straight truth!

I voted third party, we would have had had our first woman president and our first Jewish vice president. But I didn't vote to make history, I voted for what I believe is right because too many puppets can't think for themselves and vote party lines no matter what. People would vote for Hitler knowing what he did if he was a member of their political party. They would justify it saying, "I'm not Jewish so it doesn't matter to me."

On January 6th of 2021, the Capitol building in Washington DC was breached by pro Donald Trump crowds. Things got ugly and it was the first time the Capitol had been breached since the war of 1812. How did things get so ugly? Last time I was there in 2019 security was all over me whenever I tried to take pictures. They knew these people were coming but didn't stop them. Why?

Maybe because as United States citizens we have the right to take back our government and our country from the oppressors and career politicians who are sponsored by corporate America. They are the ones running the show voting for their masters. They are evil, they are vile, and they don't give a damn about any of us. They are liars, cheats, corporate puppets! Most are millionaires and get pensions for life, stipends while they're in office, more than most people make in a year busting their asses in real society to pay these clowns. All they care about is money, power, and themselves.

Our founding fathers are rolling over in their graves on how this country has turned out. They were very oppressed and wrote a nice little document declaring freedom from a colonizing government and it rings true to this day.

"We hold these truths to be self-evident, that all men are created equal, that they are endowed by their Creator with certain unalienable Rights, that among these are Life, Liberty and the pursuit of Happiness.--That to secure these rights, Governments are instituted among Men, deriving their just powers from the consent of the governed, --That whenever any Form of Government becomes destructive of these ends, it is the Right of the People to alter or to abolish it, and to institute new Government, laying its foundation on such principles and organizing its powers in such form, as to them shall seem most likely to affect their Safety and Happiness."

The government is us, the people, and when it gets too big and out of control, it's up to us to alter it or abolish it and start anew. And its past time because the people in there now have no term limits nor would they do that to themselves.

And they serve their masters. They're not at the top. They're like an iceberg, we only see 10% of what really is happening. And who really is in charge and pulling their strings?

THE USUAL SUSPECTS

Ok here we go. These are the supposed groups that control or try to control the world and every aspect of our society. I am not going to go into severe detail because I would be writing volumes of books on each subject matter. But here are the usual suspects who control our free world and a few you might not know about or have ever thought of. You've heard of many of them, the Masons, the Illuminati, the Bilderberg's, and many more.

Let's start with the Masons. Everyone's heard of the freemasons. They're everywhere. In your towns, your workplaces, your neighborhoods. People say they're a secret society, but they are just a society of secrets. There is nothing secret about them. Everyone knows one.

Many of our founding fathers were Freemasons.

They have lodges, own buildings in communities, and do lots of charitable work. They trace their roots back to the building of the pyramids.

So why do people point at them so much when talking conspiracy?

Because they don't know much about them, and they have had lots of influence throughout history. 56 men signed the Declaration of Independence and at least 9 were masons and at least 13 of the 39 that signed the Constitution were freemasons, or masons as many call them.

So thus, the conspiracies sprang up about the formation of our country based on masonic theologies. Many people believe that the Freemasons set the country up so they could rule it and they could have all the power. There have been thousands of books written about the Freemasons over the years and many people claim they are a secret society, but they are nothing but a society with secrets. They don't let just anybody enter and join and it is just like a fraternity or anything else there are a lot of initiations and a lot of rights. I do believe that they have had a lot of influence in this country and just like anything else fraternity brothers, sorority sisters, you keep those connections, and they are influenced by one another and many times when it comes to jobs, politics, anything in society people always stick together with likeminded people and that's how it goes with the Freemasons. I believe the Freemasons do not control this world; I don't think they have enough power or influence to be a worldwide group, nor do they have enough money since membership is way down. And if they are controlling the world please step up and do a better job.

THE ILLUMANITI

The illuminati were a group formed in Bavaria by Adam Weishaupt, who was a very well-educated man and was living in the time when the Catholic church controlled much of Europe through its laws in the 1770's. He was interested in enlightenment and joined the Masons but found it too expensive and not open to many of his ideas. So, he broke off and formed his new group. it basically was like the Freemasons, you had secret handshakes secret names, secret passwords, and more. They were using the group to enlighten their minds and came up with many new ideas they got many Freemasons to come to their side because they were a little more open minded. They had a lot of problems with the Freemasons and other groups. Because they did think so differently and by taking other groups members, they were taking away their money and their power. With the money and the power, they would have businesses and like Freemasons and other groups they would make money because only their members would deal with them. And they were exclusionary on things like that, so it hurt a lot of people, a lot of the poorer people per se, then it did that helped a lot of people. There was a lot of internal dissent amongst the illuminati because of the power structure and like any other organized group or even an unorganized group there is always a struggle for power and there is always somebody jealous of those at the top that feel they should be up there and doing a better job. Much of the opposition of the illuminati and Freemasons and other groups came from the Catholic Church (see a pattern here with the Catholic church and world history?) which held most of the power in Europe at that time as stated before. By not going to the church and not dealing with Catholics when they did not have to these groups put a dent in the money power of the Catholic Church. They also were in many ways anti-religious which is why they started their organizations because they did not like being told what to do by a religion that was out of touch with humans basically. It's not much different than today. You have the higher ups that are out of touch, the people in power, which try to tell those that don't have much or any power or even money what to do and how to live their lives. The old commanding the young. And the illuminati and other groups splintered away because they did not like tolerating that.

The illuminati and many of these other groups started to get political power so they had much influence when it came to voting issues and of course again, the Catholic Church was the top dog, they got scared because it was taking away from them and their power and their money. So, they decided to do something about it.

Therefore in 1785 the Catholic Church who still had a heavy influence in Bavaria convinced Duke Charles Theodore to pass an edict outlawing all secret societies. Many in these societies were rounded up and killed and their possessions were all taken by the government/Catholic Church which worked hand in hand together. Therefore, the illuminati and the Masons had to go underground but the Freemasons had expanded where the illuminati did not expand as much and pretty much were disbanded. But as of 2021 in modern day America and around the world people are still convinced the illuminati is strong and runs the world and many people believe there are symbols being used, hidden symbols in the money, in the music industry, the entertainment industry, sports, that many of these people are of fact illuminati. But most of these people have no clue what the illuminati are or were and they just call themselves that because it's good for popular culture and new world order conspiracies. Most of these people are very clueless. Yet sometimes clueless people will do anything for money. Many people still believe that the illuminati had satanic overtones and many people you see today in the music industry display these whether it's for controversy to get publicity or maybe they are exposing their truth and their real feelings.

Yet the religious groups still persecute them saying that these groups came from Satan, Lucifer, the devil, whatever you want to call him, and they claim they are non-Christian groups and that's why they don't like them.

And then the people claiming they are Illuminati get free publicity. And that's all most care about themselves and money.

THE BILDERBERGS

The Bilderberg group, I previously mentioned earlier on, or committee, started in 1954 and is an annual conference between North America and Europe elite and the group's agenda supposedly was to prevent another world war and to bolster capitalism and the free trade market around the world. Many of the participants were from all walks of upper-class life, such as politicians, and of course leaders from the industries from around the world and finance. The exact number of participants averages about 120 to 150 a year and it got its name from the 1st place it was held, the Bilderberg hotel in the Netherlands.

The meetings have fueled conspiracy theories for many years because of the people that have been known to show up there and how it is all shrouded in secrecy. The representatives are not elected but are chosen and many wonder who is at the top and is controlling things and who is doing the choosing?

2/3 of the participants are from Europe and the rest are from North America. Over the years this group has been exposed and many people find out where they are meeting and although they are not allowed on the properties certain groups including Alex Jones, a man I believe genuinely cares about America and what's really going on, has gone in, and protested at these sites and has called out some of the people that they have seen going there. They do have a committee, the chairman of the steering committee as it is called, and they are the one who comes up with their participants list. Now these are all men of wealth and power thus leading to more conspiracies. Such as what do they really talk about? Are they really gathering for the best interest of the countries or for themselves? Do they represent the people or are they there to represent their people, the rich and the powerful and the famous? The Elites of the World.

There is no transparency here and there is no accountability. So that leaves many people to wonder what exactly are they up to? Even Fidel Castro called them out saying that they were trying to create cliques and control the world and the world's economy. Now he didn't like capitalism, but he did have some immensely powerful connections and much as I do not want to agree with him, I honestly believe he was very correct. This is a group that has too much power, they have no accountability, you don't really know who goes there, you don't know what they're talking about, and why are they going there? Why isn't Russia represented or Israel?

This is an elite group of leaders and powerful men from around the world and this is the group, one of many, that we need to be made aware of and watch out for because they have a lot of power. You don't think that maybe 150 people from around this world can control this world, but it could be less than that that can because we all know money controls the world and he who has the money has all the power and that power is the ultimate aphrodisiac, and it goes straight to these people's heads!

They do not care about you or me, they are the ones to decide the finances, whether to print more money, to move on or off the gold standard. This is a group of people that you need to be awoke to and aware of. Yes, many people think "oh they're not doing anything wrong" well if they're not doing anything wrong then release your notes to us and tell us what you're doing because we as Americans have a right to know because it affects all of us around the world. This is an extremely dangerous organization! Any organization that does not have to hold any accountability to anybody above them is an extremely dangerous organization and everybody needs to be woke to this.

Like I said, there are so many groups out there like this one and if I were to write everything there is to know about these groups it would be an extra 10 books and 500 chapters. I am just writing to expose you to the corruption at the higher power and to get you to open your mind to the groups that are out there that are hurting you and this world. Awareness is part of the key, if you know what's going on and what to lookout for it helps you out a little bit. And that's what I'm hoping to do, wake people up, make them aware of what's going around in their world, to help you and help everyone.

NEW WORLD ORDER

OK, here we go with another one, the new world order as it has been coined. This phrase was made famous by former president George Herbert Walker Bush in one of his speeches. Many presidents since then have referred to this phrase and it's been referred to many times around the world with some of your more elitist of the world so to speak. Many people will call this a conspiracy theory but it's not a theory if it's true. And many conspiracy theories or so-called conspiracy theories over the years, had been proven true such as many I have spoken on earlier in this book. To get people to look bad all you must do is say the word conspiracy theory or conspiracy theorists and people right away think nut job or crazy guy. Just because you don't agree with something doesn't mean it's not true. What do you call a conspiracy theorist whose theories have come true? You call him a prophet.

Mk Ultra, poisoned alcohol by the government during prohibition, JFK assassination, Gulf of Tonkin, attacks in America to drum up support against Cuba, Iran Contra, Project Sunshine, Tuskegee Syphilis study, are just a few conspiracy theories that have been busted wide open and proven true. So, when someone says conspiracy theory don't just automatically assume it's just a theory. It might take a few years, but these things really happen, and they are usually controlled by corporations and our government. It's heartbreaking to think that a government that is designed to take care of us would study things on its own people including killing people. But they don't really care. They don't care about us they only care about certain people, they're elitist.

Ever wonder who owns the most farmland in the USA and why? Ever wonder how rich pedophiles never go to jail? Ever wonder why politicians don't get in trouble for insider trading on the stock market? Have you ever wondered how some of the most brain-dead morons you've ever seen can get elected to a public office let alone the president? It's because they are hand picked by their masters and put in power and they will serve their elite masters by doing whatever it takes because they love that money and power more than they do mankind. And their masters are the corporations because that's what America and the world has become. A New World Order Corporation.

According to the so-called conspiracies the new world order is a group of elites that want to control the world. This is nothing new. Many empires have tried to control the world and, in many ways, did with regulations on trading and meeting such as the above the Bilderberg group which controls how things get done. Many people say, "Oh how can such a small group of people control the world." You tell me how such a small group of people can control most of the monies in the world.

Leaders such as Woodrow Wilson and Winston Churchill have even used the phrase new world order. The back of the dollar bill has a pyramid with an all-seeing eye and has the Latin phrase "Novus order Seclorum" which means in English when translated basically "a new order of the ages." This has been on money since

1935 on the United States dollar bill and it's been on the great seal of America since 1782. Is this a coincidence? Not at all. This is all planned and everything going on around you right now has been planned and every now and then somebody comes on to the scene and breaks up the plan and they don't like that. Whether you want to believe it or not it's true.

Who are they? The people at the top of this world with all the money and power that are running the world that tell all of us so called little people what to do, how to think, how to feel, and what to buy. These people control the media, they control the sports teams which people go and spend tons of money on for so called entertainment but it's just a way of wasting time and controlling others just like the Gladiators back in the day. It's a distraction from what's really going on around you. The powers that be control the cars you drive, the products you buy in your home, everything!

They control the banking system including the Federal Reserve which there is nothing federal about it. The Federal Reserve is controlled by foreign nations which ends up controlling America. China owns the majority of the Federal Reserve.

Many great authors have written books about the new world order such as HG Wells, Pat Robertson, Jim Marrs, and many others. They try to expose the truth out there, but many people just blow it off because they are told to, and they believe what they are told. The American media has made Joseph Goebbels the Nazi propaganda chief immensely proud!

As long as people have their "stuff" they don't care. They don't care about the homeless, poverty, low-income housing, black lives mattering, the only time they care about this stuff is when it's trending and it can make somebody look and feel good about themselves. But a majority of the population are selfish and greedy and as long as they have their material items, they don't give a damn about anybody else! And that's just like our government. They want you to be blinded. They don't want you to care. They want you to go to work, drink your booze, do your drugs, go on your cruises, buy your possessions, and pay your taxes and be a good little boy and girl.

You ask how a small group of people could control billions around the world? Well, they're not controlling the people without controlling the nations and what controls the nations is free trade and money. And the United States is one of the worst. Have you ever wondered how such a young country such as ours has gotten so rich and powerful in just less than 250 years of actual existence? How could that be? The United States works with other countries and the United Nations to control what gets done. And there are many people that don't want the United States to succeed, and those people are sadly, many of them, are United States citizens usually the elite. We don't know why they don't want America to succeed but with all their actions it's obvious they don't, and it includes many past presidents and the current president at the time of this writing with some of the executive orders and laws they try to pass.

The United States political system is probably one of the most corrupt in the world, but it doesn't get called out for it if people have their material items. If you have your boat, your car, your fancy home, your night clubs, your country clubs, you don't care what goes on with the world. You don't care if there are people starving in the streets and neither do the elite and the new world order. The new world order is a part of the United Nations and it's happening right before your very eyes and everybody's letting it happen because everybody, well most people, are puppets. You dance when the man says dance because they give you a little bit of money and you say that's OK because I buy things. Yes, you're buying things like a Mercedes-Benz which was owned and operated and helped the Nazis, but you don't care about that you

don't care about the banks you invest
with which made money off the backs of
slaves and traded in slaves. Most only
care about yourself and that's what the
powers that be count on.

CORPORATIONS/BANKS/BIG BUSINESS

In the beginning of the United States history money always talked. Whether you were a farmer or a business owner, if you had a lot of money, you had a lot of power and influence whether it was in the community, your state, or the country. And that has not changed and over the years it has gotten much worse as far as the corporations go and the banking system. Stop and ask yourself how does a bank make so much money or how does an insurance company make so much money? If they have to payout on insurance claims, how do they make money? Well, they have over 200 million people giving them $500 a month if not more, how do you think they make money and then they come up with laws that say you must have insurance on everything or else you can't function whether it's a car or a small business or your home. Who owns those insurance companies? The corporations! They go through and they buy up everything under the sun. They control everything including the stock market. That was recently shown to society as many average working-class people started making money on the stock market and suddenly it shut down temporarily. Because they don't want the average man to make a lot of money because that way, they cannot control him and keep him down.

Who regulates the business in America? The government. They regulate it, and they make the rules, and they get kickbacks from these corporations to send business their way or to vote their way. It's corruption at the highest level and it's been that way for many years and anybody that steps up to stop it gets taken down. Whether it's with a bullet, financially, or slanderously they do get taken down because the corporations and big government all work together and they don't want anybody to get in their way.

How is it a person in the United States can become a politician with hardly any money and get into a job making $170,000 a year plus some perks yet in a couple of years have millions of dollars in the bank? Now in the meantime they still must have a house and a car and pay bills so how is it they get so rich so fast? It's because they're getting paid off. You need to realize these guys don't want to work for you, they don't care about you only your vote. They only pander to the minority community when it's voting season other than that they don't care.

You could drive through the ghetto of any big USA city and you're passing abandoned houses, empty factories and buildings, people sleeping in the street, crackheads and drug addicts, prostitutes, and people begging for money, but then you'll see a big sign saying so and so for senator, they care about you or this guy for president. They don't care about them because if they did, they would not be able to deal with what they see very well at all. But they will never see it because they never go into those communities. Because they don't care!

And the corporations over time have gotten greedier. They have sold out to the highest bidder many of them selling out to foreign interest or putting themselves on the stock market to where their stocks are bought out by foreign interests so they are no longer controlled by American companies and corporations have to appease the stockholder and do what they say that way the stockholder can make some money so to make more money they will start producing and manufacturing things overseas using slave labor or very extremely low paid might as well be slave labor and in many cases child labor. Meanwhile leaving all the United States citizens near poverty yet they still bring everything over here to sell. And they don't sell it cheap either.

And even though it's made overseas cheaper they still charge good prices over here. And to beat taxes and tariffs of imports they might build a non-union factory here and sell cars here full of foreign parts, but all that profit money goes back overseas to those companies, companies and countries that tried to kill us just a short time ago. Companies that people are supporting that built the planes that dropped the bombs on Pearl Harbor. Companies that helped kill 6 million Jewish people in a horrific Holocaust. But people don't care about that they only care about their stuff. It's a horrible game and it's disgusting, and we need to step up against the corporations and fight back and the way to fight back is to boycott their products.

But the corporations know that what they are building people need and people today, they don't have the moral ethics that they really need, and they will still buy them. Because they don't care! They don't care about the fact that Flint Michigan used to be home to the world's largest automobile factory but now it's home to the world's largest abandoned lot. When that factory left it took thousands and thousands of jobs with a ripple effect leaving a city that was already struggling in deep poverty. But people don't care because they don't live there, and they don't have to deal with it. They don't care that the majority of the population there is black folks. They like living in their ultra-white so called progressive areas with the rent and housing cost so high that it keeps the minorities out, but they claim that they are part of progressiveness and caring but saying things and doing things are two different things and they are nothing but slaves to the puppet Masters!

Greed is the name of the game, yet they will say it's capitalism so it's OK. The banks don't help much either. They are owned by the corporations and many of the banks in the United States are foreign owned banks. And although they might be charging a low interest rate that interest rate is compounded usually on a daily or monthly basis so if you buy a $300,000 home on a traditional 15-to-30-year loan you might pay anywhere from $72,000 to $155,000 in interest. Do you really think that's fair? Do you really think that's affordable Not to mention everything else extra you have to spend on like taxes, upkeep, maintenance, and more? On a $100,000 house loan at 3% interest, you will be paying approximately $52,000 in interest overtime. That's how the banks stay in business. That's how they keep you working your job. Yes, everybody needs a place to stay and a place to live but how about making things more affordable? And think about that house you bought. Let's say it costs $25,000 to make and build, and it's been sold five times and the price keeps going up so the Realtors and the bankers who work hand in hand are making money and lots of it off the backbones of hard-working Americans. And who controls all this is the corporations!

The corporations have been bought by the rich for years. Look at the names throughout time like the Rockefellers, the Bush family, DuPont, JP Morgan, Carnegie, Vanderbilt, Ford, Edison, Westinghouse, Bezos, Gates, and many more. They bought everything up and they ruined many people's lives because they would force them through bad ethics that they would have to sell. These are not good upstanding individuals like you think they are. Yes, many of them have done some charitable work but when you look past that look at what they've done. Not to mention that when they do charity work it truly is a tax deduction and it has an ulterior motive and knowing they have millions and billions of dollars they could do so much more, but they don't.

 Look at the people responsible for the Johnstown flood in Pennsylvania. It was rich people that wanted the water dammed and done cheaply so they could have a nice little lodge. This stuff still exists today like on the West Coast where you have the Bavarian club, a club full of rich people where no one's allowed to go in, and they meet there every summer. As I mentioned earlier Alex Jones, he was able to get in there and get video of some of the crazy things that went on there and these are the people that run the world and run our country. We should be worried.

Almost 50% of the global wealth in the world is owned by 1% of the people in the world and those are the rich people in the corporations and usually many of them have inherited their money and they did not work hard for it. Most of these people have never worked a hard day in their life. Oh sure, you will hear about Jeff Bezos started Amazon in his garage, but they won't tell you the fact that he got a $300,000 gift from his dad to get started. That's not working hard. That's not struggling from the ground up. I don't know about you people reading this, but I sure wish my family had $300,000 to give me to help start my business.

You grow up and hear stories about how you can make it in this world if you try and I believe you really can, but you need help along the way. And if you come up with something good somebody like Thomas Edison will try to take it from you and make it his own and destroy you in the process. I'm not saying never give up but I'm saying we need an equal playing field for everybody.

It's sad but the system is broke and to fix it we must dismantle everything from the top down. When president Donald Trump was elected in 2016, he said he was going to go in and drain the swamp and he had good intentions to do this, but I don't think he realized how deep the swamp was. Washington DC is like an iceberg you only see 10% and 90% is under the water and that is the powers that be that are controlling everything. This country was bought and sold years ago by the corporations and now thanks to President Nixon and others like him, the Chinese are big owners of this country. Now the United States government will not disclose how much money we owe China, but it is well over $1 trillion. We owe them so much money in loans. They could come in and call default on the loans and take us over and control the whole West Coast and we'd have to call it even. It's not our fault, as far as we the people go, but it's the people that we the people have elected. We don't put good people in there, people vote along party lines, and they get told what to think and feel by the next group I'm going to expose!

THE MEDIA

I could have put this in with the corporations because the media is owned by the corporations. If you go through and look and see what media outlets are owned by who and what agenda the owners have you would quickly realize that the media of the United States is all propaganda. And people used to criticize the Nazis and their propaganda, but America has done it just as long and probably even better. Why do you think so many people feel they have to dress a certain way, drive a certain car, have to be this thin, this ripped, have big breast, etc.? Because the media tells them that's how they should feel good about themselves by buying overpriced junk Made in China by slave/child labor.

Back in the day the media's job was to report the news and yes, they might have exaggerated a little bit especially during the war to make people feel better about the war effort, but things have changed a lot. There are several small media outlets out there that are independent but for the most part there are six huge corporations that own all the media worldwide! Let me reiterate that, 6 corporations that control everything you see and do.

They are national amusement owned by Sumner Redstone, Disney, Time Warner, Comcast, News Corp, and Sony. These companies own almost everything you see on tv, the internet, hear on radio, and read. Their total value combined is 430 billion dollars! That we know of.

So, do you honestly feel that you can get unbiased media in this world anymore? Do you really think they're going to tell you the truth what's going on or what they want you to believe is going on? Every day with the media dividing the country, dividing the people more and more, they want Black people against whites, they want straights against gay people, Christians against Muslims, they want everybody against the Jews, (never did understand that one and I never will). It is the oldest trick in the book divide and conquer. It's been going on for thousands and thousands of years all the way back to the days of Phillip the 2nd who used it in Greek as his motto. The reason they do this is to empower those in charge and keep those who are not in charge the so-called subjects, to keep them down to keep them from rising and getting equal.

Nicolo Machiavelli wrote about this in his book in 1521 the art of war but this is nothing new. Julius Caesar used it; Napoleon used it. It is being used right now today but most people are too ignorant to see it because they're simply happy with having their stuff, a fact I have reiterated quite a bit here for obvious reasons. And that's what the powers that be want. They want you to be complacent in society, they give you a little money now and then and give you the opportunity to make more money, but they don't give you the opportunity to make the money they do like many of these people that they have the power. They don't want you to have the power.

 Look at all the politicians in our country. They get in there and they're millionaires, how is that? Because they're taking kickbacks from the corporations. Oh, sorry it's called "campaign contributions." They don't give it back if they lose. These are the same people that want to outlaw guns yet everybody that's out there protecting them has a gun and they have private security details.

These are people that want to change the constitution. They want to change it because they say it's outdated because they know it's a good document. Our founding fathers did not have a lot of government set up; they knew what they were doing. But if they keep you hating one another it makes it easier for them to control you plain and simple. Most people are being controlled and they are nothing but puppets. Many of them don't see it.

And then they try to rewrite history. They don't teach real history in the schools anymore. They teach what they want them to believe. They don't tell them the truth. And who puts the schoolbooks out? The corporations and the media that all work hand in hand because all the schools buy their books from the same companies. So, if you read the same misinformation over and over, you're going to believe it and then you will discredit those that know the truth. Those that truly know and have experienced the reality. The schools are nothing but indoctrination stations anymore that's why so many kids are getting home schooled now.

It's just like during Black History Month what do they teach them? Doctor Martin Luther King Junior, maybe Frederick Douglass or Harriet Tubman that's about it. You won't hear about Medgar Evers or Emmett Till or a lot of people that gave their lives for the cause unwillingly. And they definitely won't teach you about Malcom X. And then during Juneteenth what do you hear? Not much. The same thing and most people seem to forget about it especially when it's over. And they tell you this is what happened.

Martin Luther King Junior Day in January in the United States is a federal holiday, and you'll see ads on television and a lot of folks making post about him on social media and quoting him. But then you don't see or hear much until January of the next year unless someone can somehow invoke his great name and use it to their advantage, say to get elected to public office.

I recently was down at the Lorraine motel in Memphis doing my own investigation and I do not believe for one minute that James Earl Ray killed Doctor Martin

Luther King junior. I don't believe it. I never have and never will. But that's what they want you to believe. None of it adds up but they will tell you that's what happened so you will believe it. Who killed John F. Kennedy? Lee Harvey Oswald? Not at all, but you can't really find out the truth when you kill the people that are being suspected of things. But that's what they preach to everybody that this is the way it is, and this is the truth because we said so and that just makes the people that believe in it indoctrinated little puppets.

This country is ours it was founded with the people for the people of the people. Recently current president of the United States Joe Biden said that "we the people is the government." That is not true at all but there are people that will believe it because they want the government to take care of them because they don't want to do anything or have to think and feel for themselves, they don't mind being controlled just like Pavlov's dog, ring the bell, get a treat. That's what they do to these people, they ring a little bell; they give them a little treat and they keep them appeased so these people will do whatever they're told by the government. It's 1984 come true. It's the Network come to pass.

This is the United States of America and we the people are the people. It's our country and we need to unite and take it back. The first thing we need to do is stand up to the government and unite because it's true, united we stand divided we fall!

THE TRUTH IS OUT THERE

The United States of America has been so heavily involved with corruption since its formation. In the beginning the founding fathers had a limited sense of government, meaning they did not want this government to be too big and they did not want it to be too powerful, they did not want Kings and Queens. We had already rebelled against that. That's why the constitution does not have as many laws as many countries do. As a matter of fact, ours is one of the smallest constitutions in the world. Now again, how is it that our country could be so young yet be one of the richest most powerful nations in the world? That's because capitalism has given way to the almighty dollar and the corporations like I stated earlier and as stated several many times they control this country. In the

1970s Richard Nixon opened our country to trade with China. China uses child labor and forced labor. China also has reeducation camps as they call them. But most people out there don't care they only care about the stuff they can get for free or for cheap because it's all about saving a buck and with the corporations it's all about making a lot of bucks.

I have been all around this world. I have been all around this country and I talk to anyone and everyone. I have seen ships rolling in from other countries whose names I've never heard of and whose names I cannot even pronounce, and I will talk to the dockworkers. I will ask them what they brought, and they'll tell me, and they'll also tell me that almost 80% of those ships leave our ports with nothing! They are dead heading back to countries and not taking any American made products with them. How are we able to compete with these other countries? They don't even buy our stuff. You walk into any convenience store, any Walmart, Dollar General, Family Dollar you will see that probably 90% of the stuff there is made in foreign nations. And you then wonder why your neighbors and your brothers, and your sisters can't get a job or a good paying job or why the rents are so high. It's all part of a scam, a major scam to control the masses. They don't care about you, and they don't care about me! Politicians don't care about us; all they care about is votes and money. You got people doing the same job for 50 years, yet nothing gets done. I walk into the heart of the Detroit ghetto, and I am driving past abandoned buildings, crackheads, prostitutes, people sleeping in the streets, and then I will see a brand-new sign wanting you to vote for this guy for the US Senate. This is a man that only comes out every couple years to get the black man's vote but he doesn't do anything while he was in there or is in there to help the black man or the community. Look around the community, what the hell has he done to help? Not a damn thing and they won't even go into that community because they are scared. Do you know why I go into that community? Because those are my brothers and sisters. And my people need me. And they need you too.

Those are the forgotten people of the United States that nobody gives a damn about. Well, some of us still care and we will do what we can when we can to help the brothers and sisters. But we do it privately unlike many people who must stroke their own ego and take a picture of themselves giving a dollar to a homeless man to make themselves look and feel good about things. That's the only time many people do a good deed is when they get recognized for it. A good deed should be its own reward.

Many of you sit in your $300,000 plus home in your all-white community but you go out and you say black lives matter, but you keep it to where the black people can't afford to live in your community with your systemic racism. You are a part of the problem and you people make me sick. You won't send your kids to the inner-city schools because you're scared. But I know a lot of doctors, lawyers, and Indian Chiefs from the suburbs that send their kids to the inner-city schools because they want them to learn, they want them to be with other people of different walks in life because that's what makes you a better person when you understand those people. And maybe you could help those people, maybe you can learn from those people, maybe you could step up and do something or help them advance. I'm sick and tired of the things I see in this country and that's why I stepped up and I'm writing this book and I'm telling you the truth today. I speak nothing but the truth and I always will. I stand with my brothers and sisters. I don't care what religion you are, what color you are, how much money you have or don't have, if you're a good person and you seek and speak the truth you are one of my people and that's what we all need to do. We all need to unite and that's the only way this country will ever get back on track again. We need to stand together and unite and fight for our freedoms or we're all going to be dead and die as slaves and that's what the powers that be want. They could give a damn less about me or you, they just want our money, our tax dollars, they want us programmed to go to work and be their slaves with just a little bit of pay to make it to where you can't really say we're slaves.

But most people they won't step up or do anything. They don't want to rock the boat because they just like being in the boat. They like that money. They like their material possessions. They don't care where they came from. They don't care if they were created by Nazis and Nazi owned companies in the past. They could care less about that if they get a good deal. Most people in the United States have no real morals or values. They go to church, they claim to be Christians, yet they judge other people, they judge other religions that think different than them.

They don't accept other people that think different than them. They sit there and they based their religious beliefs on Judaism in what they call the Old Testament, yet they pick and choose what laws of Moses they follow, the laws given to Moses by G-d in the so-called Old Testament. Yet they break most of those laws, but they'll judge others because they say Jews don't believe Jesus is the Messiah, so we don't accept them. They say Jews killed Jesus, so they must be bad. They will say it says in the Old Testament homosexuality is a sin, so they are against it, yet it also says you shouldn't wear a man's clothes, but I see those women wearing jeans. You don't mix materials but they're not wearing all cotton. What? What kind of whackadoodle religion are you making up people? You're making it up as you go along and that's called a cult.

They exclude people from their own communities or when they do let them in its only because they have something to present and give to them and then when it's gone, they don't care about you anymore. I see this daily. We live in the most selfish heartless times I've ever seen or heard of in my lifetime and many other lifetimes people. And I will point the finger at you, I will point the finger at the fat cats, the people who are just so complacent in life they don't care. They only care about themselves. If you want to be a puppet that's on you but I don't dance for the man or nobody!

I refuse to be a puppet I refuse to be a slave it's time we step up and take our country back. United we stand divided we die!

UNITE AND FIGHT

Sometimes I think our country is too far gone. Our world is too far gone because we are basically paid slaves. They train you to do something, they throw a little money your way and if you don't do it, they get rid of you and take that money so you will walk the line and you will do whatever they say to keep that money and your possessions. Some of us are happy and grateful with the homes that we have, and we don't need all the fancy things in this world, but others are driven for it because they must keep up with the Joneses per se for appearances sake. They feel so insecure they must have bigger and better than everybody else, yet they don't have a dime to their name because everything's on credit. Everything has been financed so technically they are broke, and they owe everybody. But nobody knows that except them, so they still look and feel good and look down and judge others.

But that's part of the game the biggest part of the game. If people could just be complacent and grateful and happy for the little things, they have in this world it would be a much better place. We are a society driven by greed and selfishness. Many say it's human nature and they believe it because they are told that and programmed to believe it. But it's not human nature! It is not human nature to be that way at all, it's human nature to be kindhearted and help lift others up instead of tearing them down. I don't believe we are that far gone as a society. I know we are tracked daily by our phones, our computers, our cars, our smart televisions. Have you under wondered why we went from the old school TV's which were fine to HD smart TV's? Think about it. Was it because technology got better? Yes, it did but better for who, us or them?

We don't have the freedoms we used to have because there are cameras on every corner taking pictures of us getting our license plates looking for traffic violations. There are red light cameras, there are speeding cameras. Freedom is really gone but you let it go because you feel it's OK in the name of so-called security. What can we do to take our country, our lives, and our world back people?

We must get back to a state of humanity. We all need to be united. That is the first step. Throw out your racism and your prejudice. Learn to love your brothers and your sisters. Do you know how many people I know that don't even know their neighbors' names or anything about them? Why is that? Because people just don't care anymore and until we get together and start caring we are doomed.

Our country was set up in many positive ways. It was not perfect because there's been a lot of bad things that happened along the way but we as a society have learned from them and corrected those mistakes and hopefully, we make sure those will never happen again such as slavery and driving the Indians/natives off their own land. Also, in 1882 there was the Chinese Exclusion Act that Congress passed which was a law that explicitly banned Chinese laborers from immigrating and obtaining United States citizenship. Most Chinese who were already residents in the United States had the dilemma of either stay in the United States alone or go back to China be with their families and were basically kicked out of the country. After coming here, facing much prejudice, and giving their lives to build the railroads they were treated like dirt and our government passed the law outlawing them. It was not until the Magnuson act in 1943 when this was ended but the damage was done. After Pearl Harbor they rounded up all the Japanese or anybody with Japanese descent and put them in concentration camps here in America. Everything I am saying is the truth and I'm telling you the truth so you can learn from it, and it will never happen again. Hopefully.

We need to quit putting politicians in office who only have their own interests at heart. That's easier said than done but we need to get rid of the two-party system, it is a joke! Yes, there are always going to be bad politicians. But we need to make sure that we research who these people are because most of them are controlled by money and corporations, or they would not be in the position they are in and once they are elected their true colors come out of who got them there and they're not going to cross those people. The political system in America is a joke.

I research the people running for office. Many people seem to forget that we are paying their salaries and that they work for us. We are their bosses! They are elected officials appointed by us to do a job to represent us. Not the special interest group that's throwing money their way, but the people and we are the people. And when we start to realize that we will get this country back people.

We need to be united; I mean after all it is the first word in the name of the country the United States of America. We need to take this country back and we all need to unite as one. That is the only way we will ever get this country back into our hands again and we need to regulate the corporations. There is no reason that a billion-dollar corporation pays no taxes. We need to start remembering humanity and helping each other out and if you have extra money help your neighbor, help your friends, help total strangers but just help others. Until we do that we are doomed as a human race. The key word is we need to unite as one and take back this country. It's we the people, for the people, by the people, and we are the people! Let's step up and do this!

Let's be better human beings and take care of mother earth. If we start there the rest will follow. We need to be more self-sufficient and more dependent on small businesses and small farmers. They are our neighbors, and we need to help them and support them. This is the only way we will ever take our country back. It all starts with awareness which I have made you very aware of everything going on now it's up to you to rise and take this country back people!

.